Sporty Riddles

Joanne E. Bernstein and Paul Cohen

Pictures by Paul Harvey

ALBERT WHITMAN & COMPANY, NILES, ILLINOIS

Also by Joanne E. Bernstein and Paul Cohen

Creepy, Crawly Critter Riddles
Grand-Slam Riddles
Happy Holiday Riddles to You
More Unidentified Flying Riddles
Riddles to Take on Vacation
Unidentified Flying Riddles
What Was the Wicked Witch's Real Name?
  and Other Character Riddles

Text © 1989 by Joanne E. Bernstein and Paul Cohen
Illustrations © 1989 by Paul Harvey
Published in 1989 by Albert Whitman & Company,
5747 West Howard St., Niles, Illinois 60648
Published simultaneously in Canada
by General Publishing, Limited, Toronto
All rights reserved. Printed in the U.S.A.
10 9 8 7 6 5 4 3 2 1

Library of Congress Cataloging-in-Publication Data
Ber
  Spo   Bernstein and Paul Cohen:
Illustrated by P
    p.   cm.
    Summary: A collection of   ts riddles,
including "What's the most ta   kking."
    ISBN 0-8075-7590-9 (lib. bdg.).
    1. Riddles, Juvenile.   2. Sports—Juvenile humor.   3. Wit
and humor, Juvenile.   [1. Sports—Wit and humor.   2. Riddles.]
I. Cohen, Paul. 1945-   II. Harvey, Paul. 1926-   ill.
III. Title.
PN6371.5.B3994   1989   89-5294
818'.5402—dc19   CIP
                                                 AC

To my mother, a terrific sport. She needed to be.   P.C.

Net Profits

How do you go fishing for a basket?
With a hook shot.

What do you call it when you throw a chicken through the hoop?
A fowl shot.

Which New York basketball players always cut themselves shaving?
The Nicks.

What New York Met and Los Angeles Laker make a delicious combination?
Strawberry and Kareem.

Why can't you keep a good basketball player down?
He'll always rebound.

What do you call a basketball team that gets shut out?
A hoopless case.

Why do basketball players have bad table manners?
They're always dribbling.

Why don't basketball players like their work?
It makes them throw up.

What <u>is</u> a basketball, anyway?
A fancy dance party in a basket.

Going Batty

How is a catcher like a dog?
He wears a muzzle, snaps at flies, and chases fowls.

What do catchers eat their dinner on?
Home plate.

How can you win a baseball game without throwing a ball?
Just throw strikes.

What position would a pig play on a baseball team?
Short slop.

How does a baseball player keep a good grip on his bat?
By holding onto its wings.

What do you get when you cross a lizard with a baseball player?
An outfielder who catches flies with his tongue.

Soccer to Me!

Why did the soccer player flood the field?
The coach asked her to come in as a sub.

What kind of lollipop does Pelé like?
An all-day soccer.

What position would a monster want to play on a soccer team?
Ghoulie.

Gym-Dandy Riddles

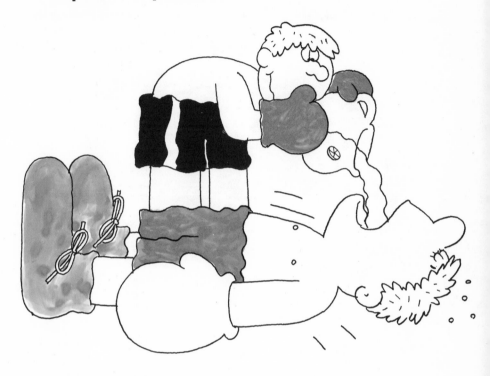

What drink do boxers like the least?
Punch.

When is a wrestler like a king's chair?
When he's thrown.

Why does it take forever to lift a twenty-foot barbell?
That's a long, long weight!

What did the wrestler's boyfriend give her?
A new pin.

They're Off and Punning!

When did the jockey decide on a career?
On the spur of the moment.

How do you saddle a racehorse?
It depends on which way you're going.

What's a jockey's favorite food?
The Belmont Steaks.

Why'd they bring a horse to the synagogue?
They needed a canter.

What do you call a comic on horseback?
A jokey.

How many legs does a racehorse have?
Six: forelegs and hindlegs.

What horse races worldwide and shoots baskets?
A globe trotter.

Goofie Golf

Why did the golfer need two pairs of pants?
In case he got a hole in one.

Why did the rich man put a baseball field on the edge of his golf course?
He wanted a diamond in the rough.

What course has the most water?
The Golf of Mexico.

Why was the golfer arrested for shooting Par?
He also shot Mar.

Why was the golfer afraid of the pizza man?
He had an <u>awful</u> slice!

Why do golfers often visit playgrounds?
For the good swings there.

Why are a golfer's pants so neatly pressed?
He always carries an iron.

It Sno Joke!

What should a skater's fiancé give her?
An engagement rink.

How many carats do you figure it should be?
Figure eight.

What sport should a skier take up if her gloves are always wearing out?
Bad mitten.

Which skater tells the best jokes?
Katarina Witt.

What's the skier's favorite lunchmeat?
Slalomi.

And what do you call a skier with seven veils?
Slalome.

Where do you go to buy cheap sleds?
You go toboggan basements (bargain basements).

What's the hardest thing about learning to skate?
The ice.

Just for Kicks

What is green with stripes, has three hundred feet, and gets stepped on by people?
A football field.

Who carries football shoes in a bag on his shoulder?
Santa Cleats.

What position would a whale play in football?
Humpback.

Why don't skeletons play football?
They don't have the guts.

Hokey Hockey

What sport does a student like to play?
Hooky.

How did they penalize the hockey player when he entered the airplane?
They gave him two minutes for boarding.

What penalty do you get for bringing an unfrosted cake to the game?
Icing.

How do hockey players kiss?
They pucker up.

What a Racket!

What can you serve but not eat?
A tennis ball.

Why is tennis such a noisy game?
The players all raise a racket.

What kind of bandage improves your serve?
An ace bandage.

Why are fish such bad tennis players?
They're afraid to get near the net.

What's the best age to learn a racket sport?
Tenish.

What did Steffi's fans paint on the walls?
Graf-itti.

Track Ticklers

Why did the bald man take up running?
He wanted to get some fresh hair.

What do you call it when a runner forgets how many times he's gone around the track?
Memory laps.

Which track event produces the most injuries?
Hurtles.

Riddles to Work Out

How do smart students get exercise?
By pursuing their studies.

What's the favorite candy in the school gym?
Recess pieces.

Does exercise kill germs?
Yes, but first you have to make the germs put on their sweatsuits.

Motorific Riddles

What do you get when you cross a motorcycle with a riddle book?

A Yamahaha.

What happened to the car racer who ate a watermelon?

He had to make a pit stop.

How does a stock car driver lose weight?

He goes on a crash diet.

What game show makes motorcycle racers rich?

"Wheel of Fortune."

Wheel Funny!

What song do elderly bikers like?
"The Old Spokes at Home."

Is biking always popular?
No, it tends to run in cycles.

Why did the silly cyclist stick his tires out the window?
They needed more air.

O-limp-yucks

Which Olympic event is the witch's favorite?
The decackle-on.

What does Grete do before the marathon begins?
Grete Waitz.

What is a three-hour opening sports ceremony?
Olympic torch-ure.

How do Olympic sportscasters get paid?
So much announce (an ounce).

Who is the world's worst gymnast?
Mary Lou Rotten.

What feat did the Austrian gymnast perform?
"The Blue Danube Vaults."

Who participates in the riflery events?
Only contestants of the right caliber.

Why did the gymnast take his bankbook with him to the meet?
He didn't want to lose his balance.

What song do Australian gymnasts sing?
"Vaultsing Matilda."

Where do you find parallel bars in the army?
On a captain.

Alley Oops!

How do we know bowling alleys are quiet?
You can hear a pin drop.

What's the only split a bowler doesn't mind?
The kind with a banana in it.

Why did the artist bring his pictures with him to the bowling alley?
He heard he could get ten frames for a dollar.

What TV program stars a hockey player and a bowler?
"Skate and Alley."

Why did the bowler bring two balls to the alley?
So she'd always have a spare.

Why couldn't the fussy bowler find a perfect ball?
They all had holes in them.

These Are All Wet

What do you call a frightened snorkler?
Chicken of the Sea.

What happens when you swim in heavy traffic?
You slow down to a crawl.

Why did the swimmer finish last?
She took a nose dive.

What's the most talkative sport?
Kayakking.

Why was the silly water-polo player so upset?
His horse couldn't swim.

Why did the long-distance swimmer watch the BBC?
She was interested in the English Channel.

Knock, knock.
Who's there?
Canoe.
Canoe who?
Canoe come out and play?

Oddballs

Is it a good idea to fish with a permit?
Yes, but a worm works better.

What game does Chevrolet hate?
Dodgeball.

What is a cardplayer's favorite sport?
Shuffleboard.

Why did all the people go to the billiard parlor on a hot summer day?
The sign in the window said, "Try our indoor pool."

What insect likes outdoor sports?
The frisbee.

Who plays cricket with a broomstick?
The Wicket Witch.

Why do volleyball players get dizzy?
They're always rotating.

How does Porky Pig's bicycle race end?
That's all, spokes!

Paul Cohen believes that the year has two seasons: baseball and winter.

Joanne Bernstein likes walking, cycling, and folk dancing— possible in all seasons.

Paul Harvey has illustrated many books for children and hopes to illustrate many more.

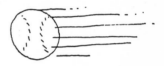